Fiddle Time Sta

Kathy and David Blackwell

illustrations by John Eastwood

© Oxford University Press 1998
Music Department
OXFORD UNIVERSITY PRESS
Great Clarendon Street, Oxford OX2 6DP

198 Madison Avenue, New York, NY10016, USA

Introduction

Congratulations! You're learning the violin. Some people think that doing this is as hard as climbing Mount Everest—but not with *Fiddle Time Starters*.

In this book you'll find . . .

- lots of rhythms to play on your violin:

Your teacher may write something next to each symbol to help you remember them.

- the down bow and up bow sign: ⊓ down bow V up bow
these signs tell your bow which direction to go in.

- charts for your left hand to show you where to put your 1st, 2nd, and 3rd finger. All the tunes in this book use this finger pattern.

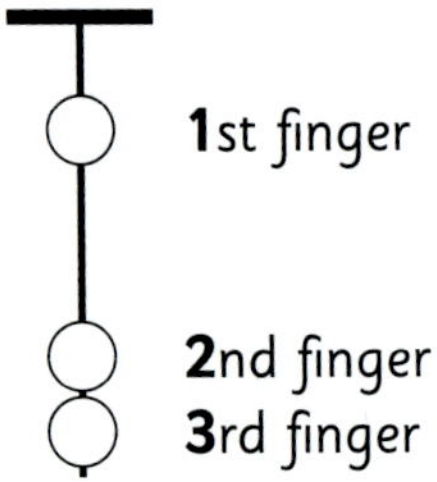

- the letter names of the notes on each string (there are only 7 to learn!):

  A B C D E F G

- the sharp sign #

- puzzles to do — have a pencil ready

- and finally, lots and lots of tunes to play.

In case you drop your book on the way to the top, write your name here:

And now, it's time to get started . . . !

Rhythm zones

- Clap and say the words of each rhythm.
- Choose a rhythm and play it several times on each open string:
  Ⓖ Ⓓ Ⓐ Ⓔ
- Play a rhythm *pizzicato*—that means plucking.
- Try another *arco*—that means with the bow.

Take off with some **Space Rhythms**

Blast off in - to space

Deep in space

Moon bug - gy

As - ter - oids and sat - el - lites

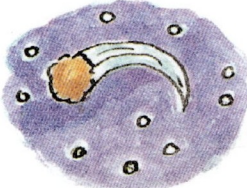

Play some hot **Jungle Rhythms**

Mis-chiev-ous mon - keys

Ti - gers and e - le-phants

An - gry al - li - ga-tors

Rat - tle snake

Slow py -thon

Jun - gle heat, jun - gle beat

Keep fit with some **Sporty Rhythms**

Rea - dy, stea - dy, go now

Quick run - ner, fast sprin - ter

Have a rest!

Dive in the deep end

Open strings

Boogie on down

Just play each string 8 times

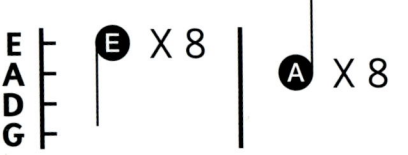

draw your bow quickly
over all four strings!

Going up

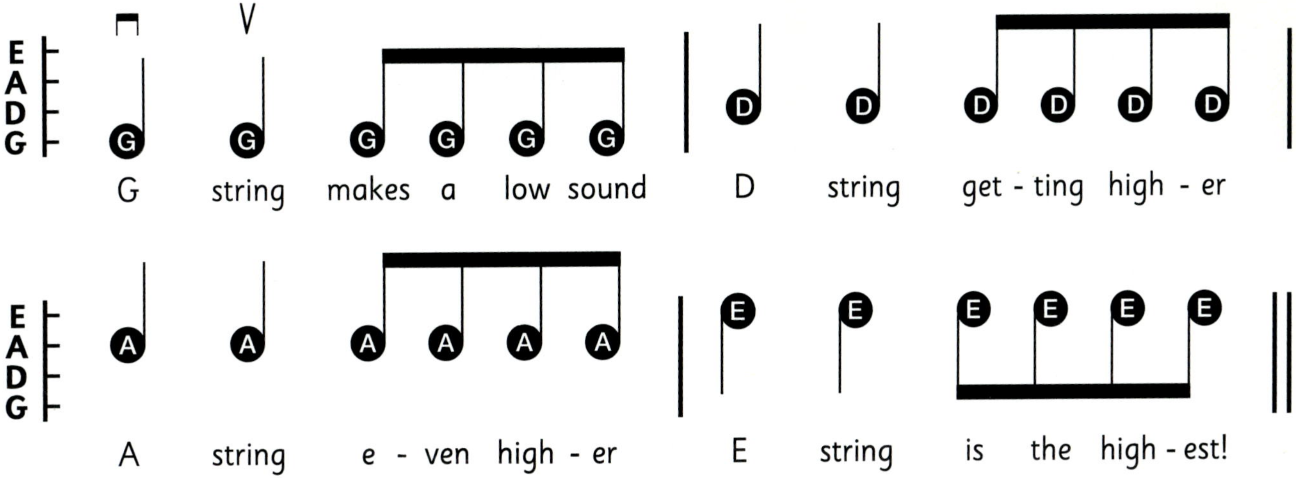

G string makes a low sound D string get-ting high-er

A string e-ven high-er E string is the high-est!

D string notes

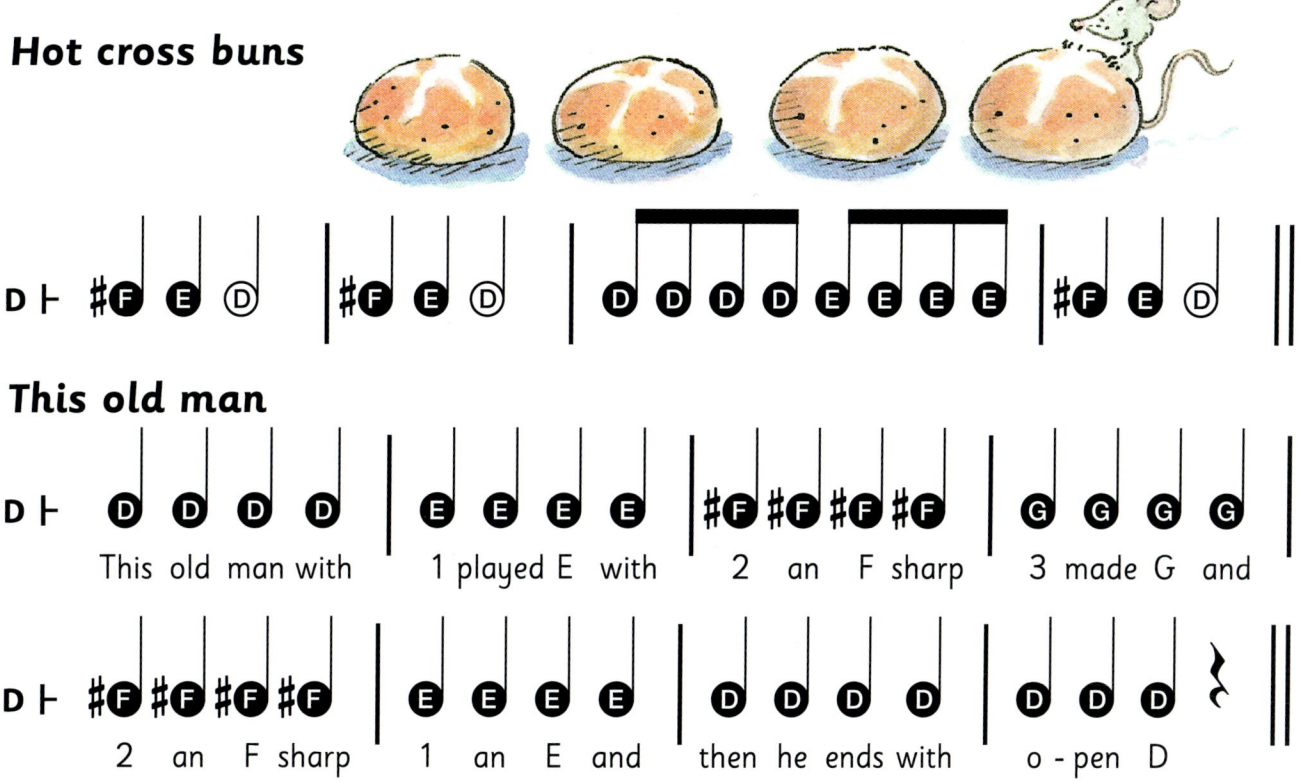

Match the rhythms to the words! Draw a line from each word to the rocket with the rhythm that fits the word.

Rocket Launcher

Moon

Astronaut

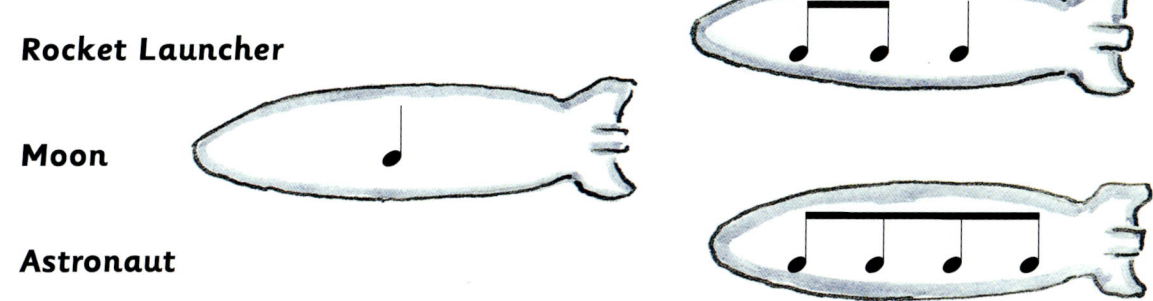

Make up some more space rhythms of your own.

Choose a space rhythm from the rhythm zone on page 4 and play it on the D string notes.

A string notes

1st finger makes the note **B**

2nd finger makes the note **C#**

3rd finger makes the note **D**

Au clair de la lune

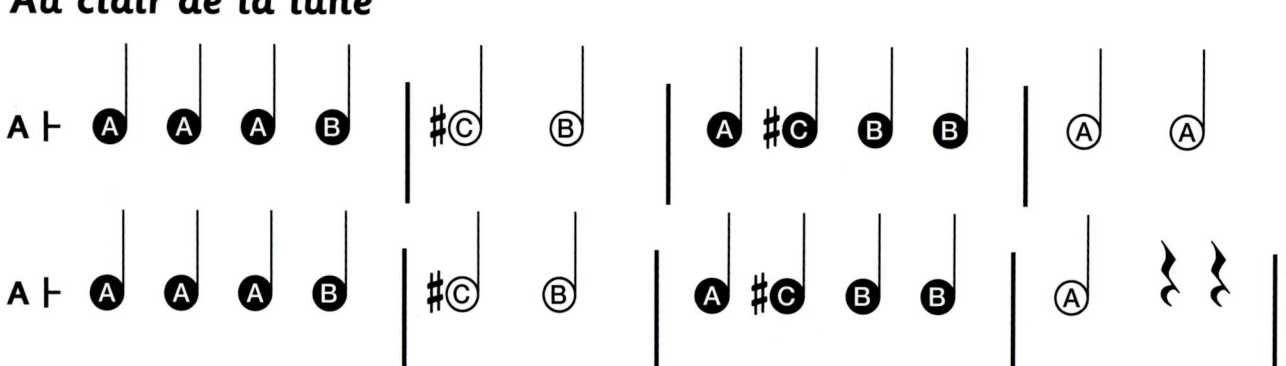

14

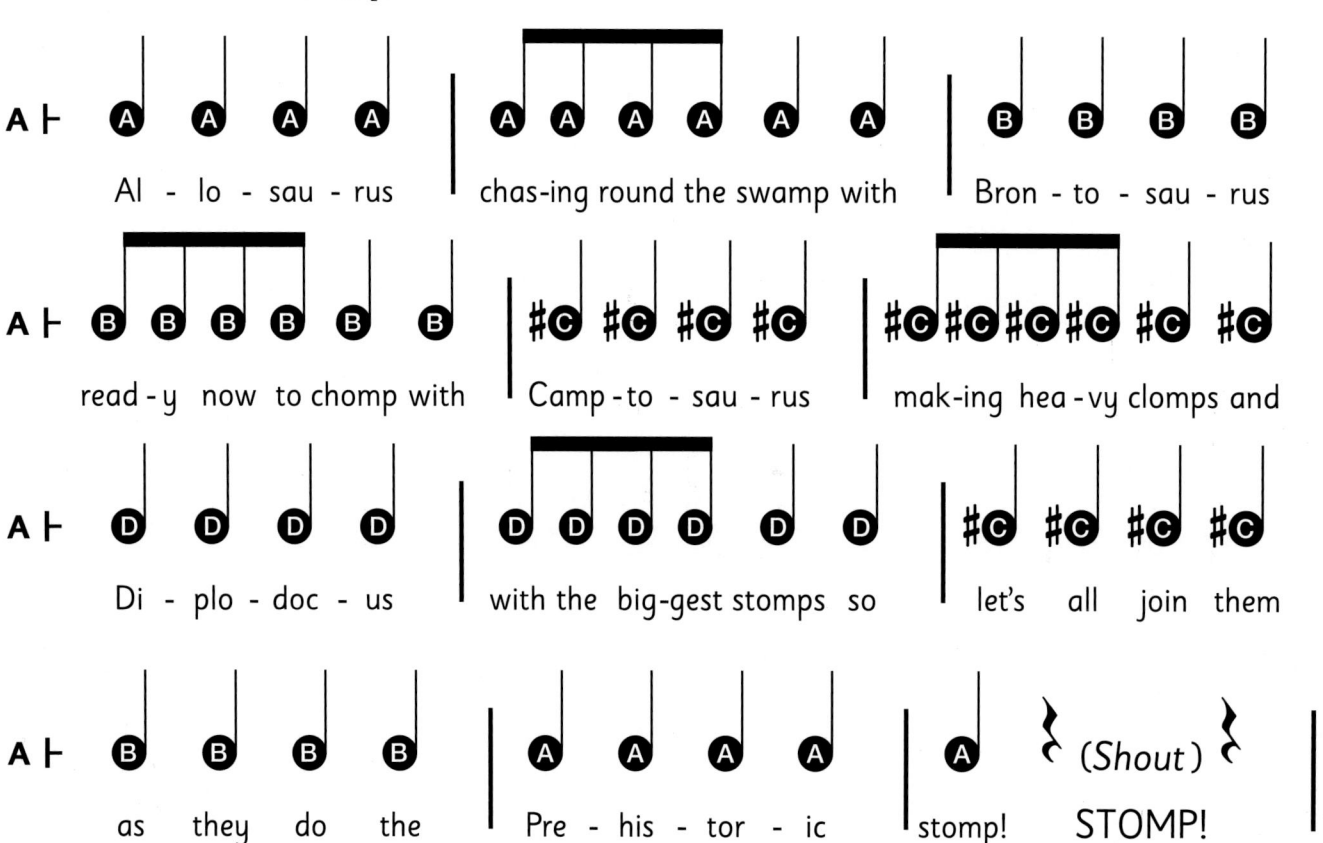

E string notes

1st finger makes the note **F#**

2nd finger makes the note **G#**

3rd finger makes the note **A**

Double click

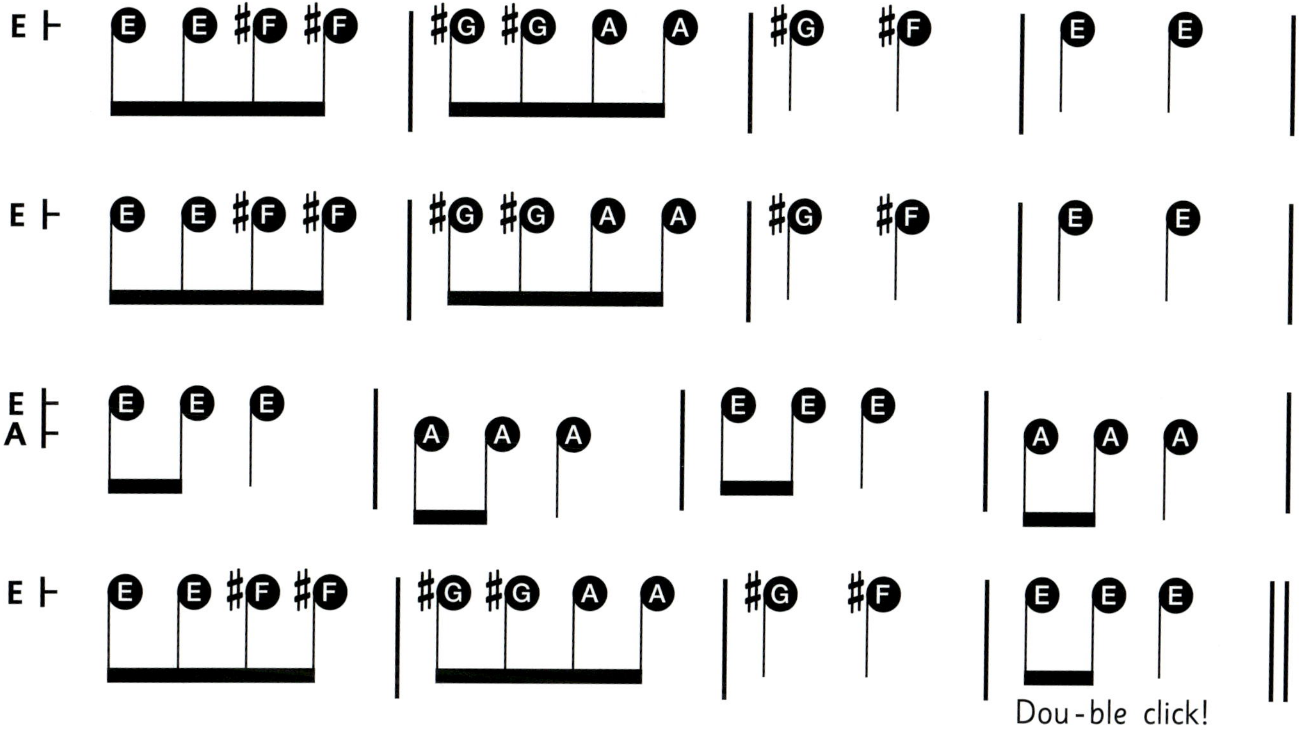

Dou-ble click!

19

Use the letter names of the E string notes to crack the computer's passwords.

			and				and			
0	2	2		3	2	0		1	0	0

Write the rhythms to fit the computer words in the boxes below.
The rhythms you need are scattered around the box.

mouse mat	
internet	
colour printer	
mega byte	
keyboard	
compact disc	

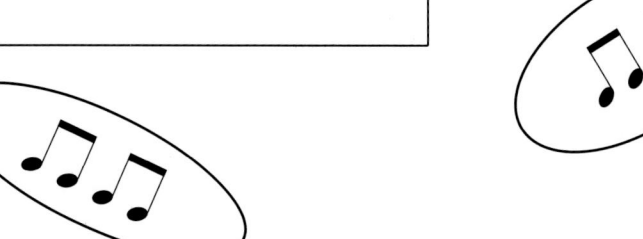

20

Mary had a violin

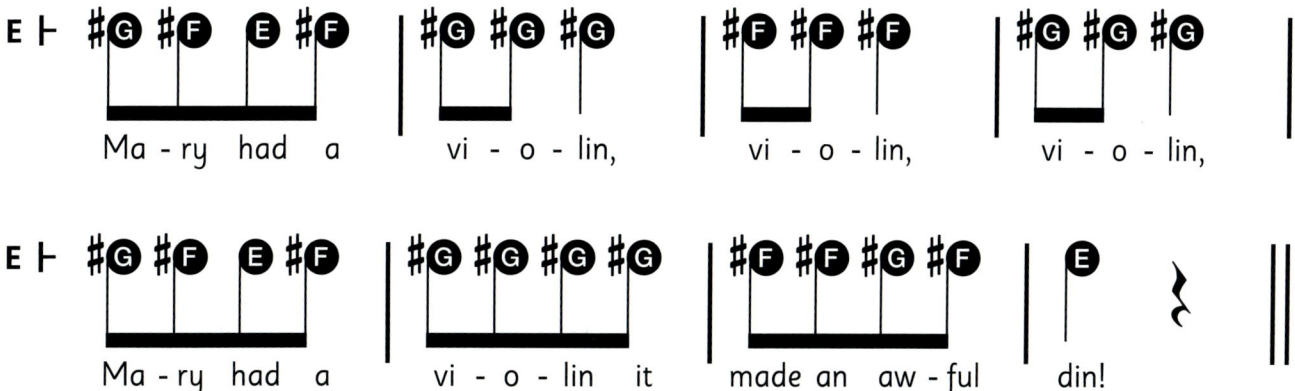

Choose a rhythm from the rhythm zones on pages 4 and 5 and play it on each of the E string notes in turn.

G string notes

1st finger makes the note **A**

2nd finger makes the note **B**

3rd finger makes the note **C**

Sleeping Lions

Go and tell Aunt Dinah

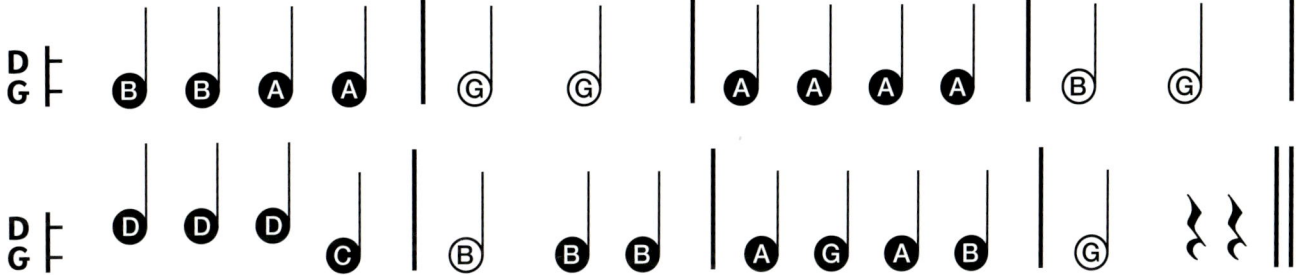

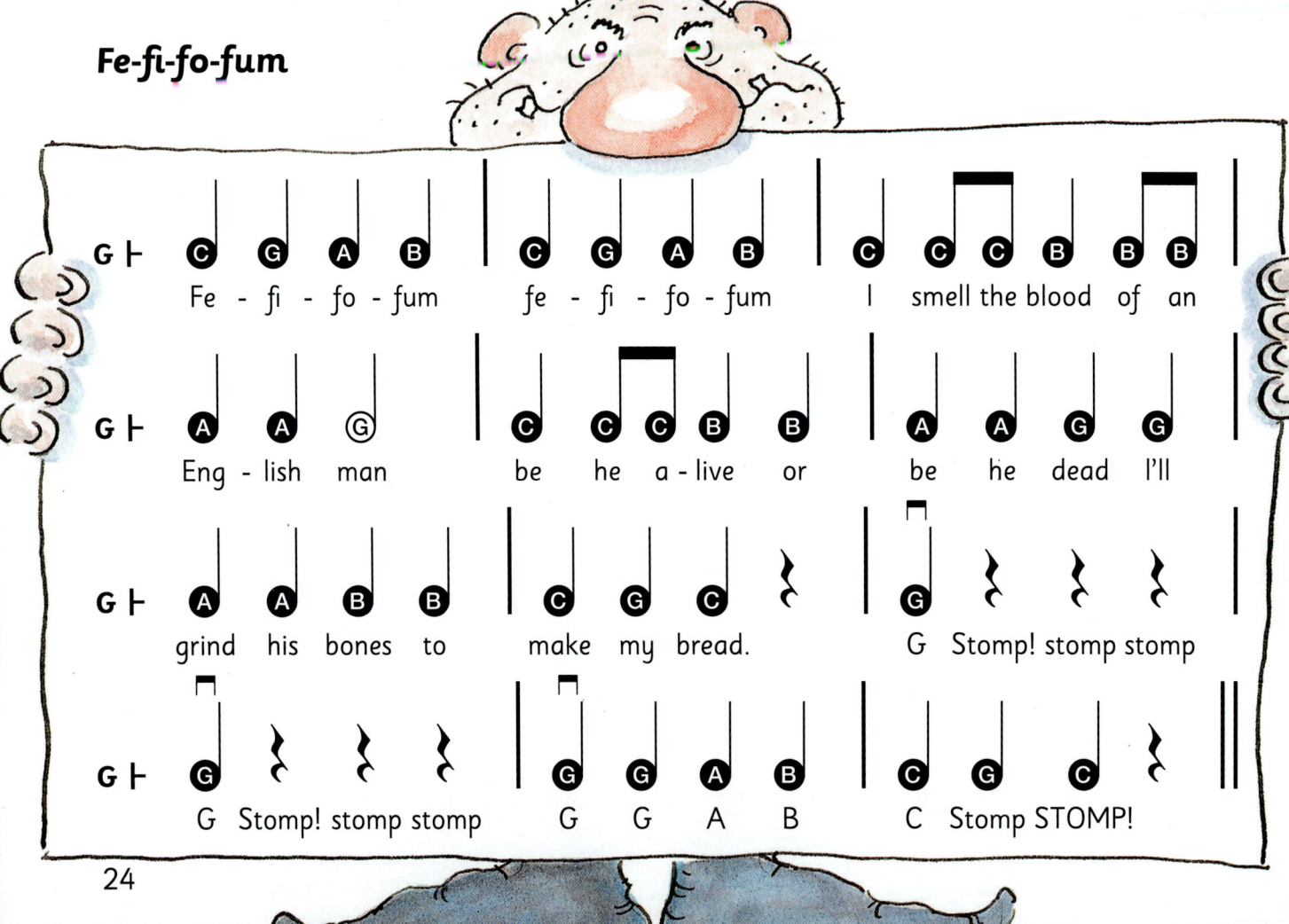

Twinkle, twinkle little star

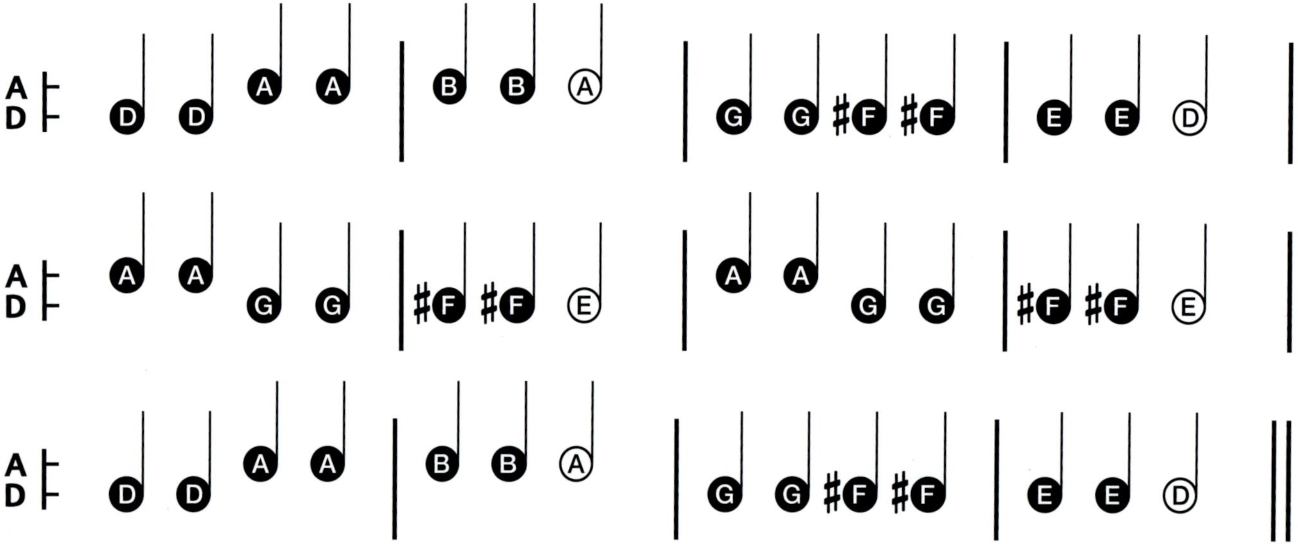

Lightly row

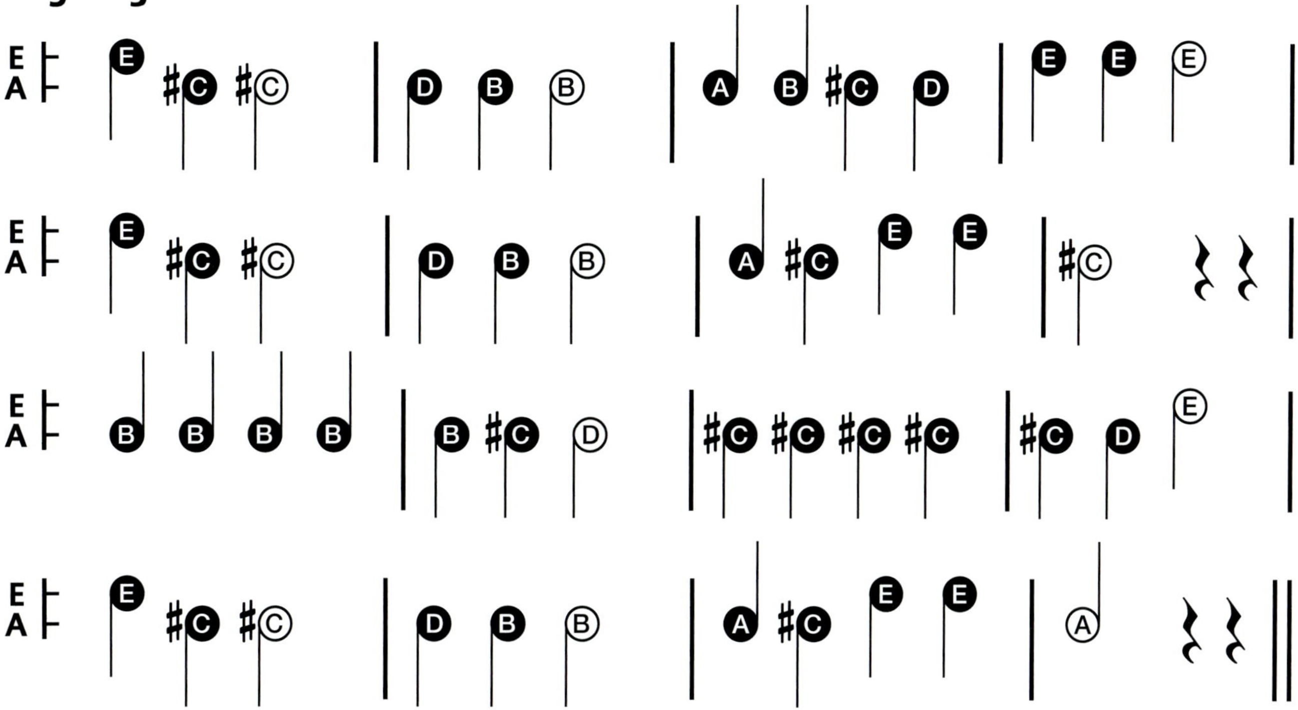

Love somebody

London's burning

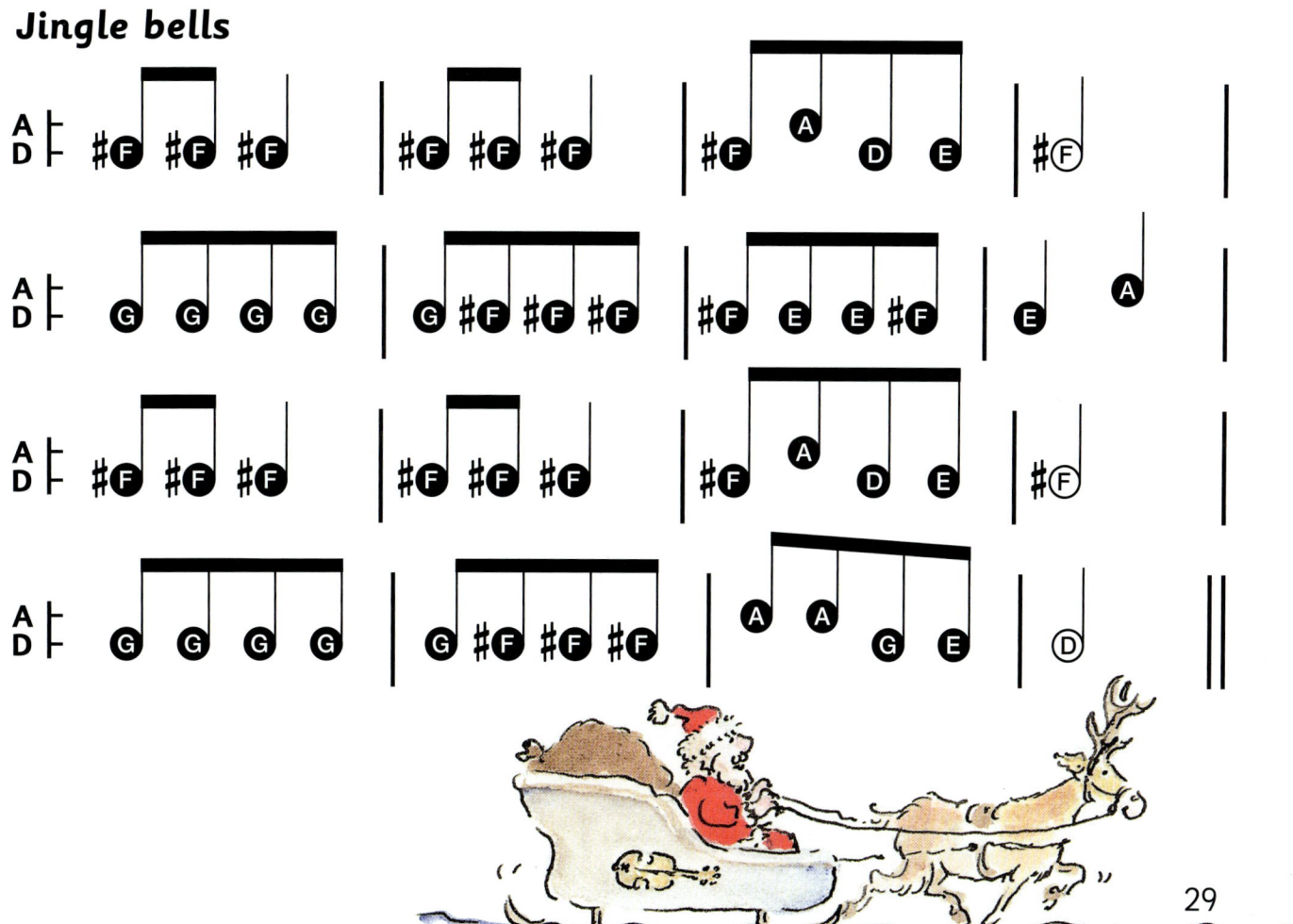

CERTIFICATE

Awarded to:

_____

for being a brilliant *Fiddle Time Starter!*

signed_____ (my teacher)

date_____

CONGRATULATIONS

Now on to *Fiddle Time Joggers*